For most of her working life Colleen Laybourne-Smith has held managerial positions within the beauty and fragrance industry, including 16 years with Givenchy. She is also a fully trained make-up artist and fragrance expert. She lives in Oxfordshire.

THE TALES OF MR AND MRS BARTHOLOMEW FOX

Written and illustrated by

Colleen Laybourne-Smith

Book Guild Publishing
Sussex, England

First published in Great Britain in 2011 by
The Book Guild Ltd
Pavilion View
19 New Road
Brighton, BN1 1UF

Typesetting in Century Schoolbook by
Keyboard Services, Luton, Bedfordshire

Printed in Spain under the supervision of
MRM Graphics Ltd, Winslow, Bucks

A catalogue record for this book is available from
The British Library

ISBN 978 1 84624 588 6

CONTENTS

v

THE DAY THE BADGERS WERE INVITED TO LUNCH

'Today, Mrs Fox, I think we'll have our lunch
    upon the lawn.'
'Oh Mr Fox! How pleasant dear!' said his wife
    with a little yawn.
'It's early yet, dear Mr Fox, so I have time to
    see
If our larder is quite full of food as we will need
    plenty.'

'And Mrs Fox I think 'twould be the nicest thing
    to do
To invite our friends the Badgers, so they can
    be there too.'
So Mrs Fox she hurried off to search her pantry
    store,
While Mr Fox went to the Badgers who only
    lived next door.

The Badgers were all very pleased, 'We'd be
    delighted to attend!
You really are a generous fox and such a special
    friend!
And what I think, dear Mr Fox, would make
    our lunch more fun
Is that if we provide the music, we can all dance
    in the sun!'

1

'Oh what a splendid thing my friend!' said Mr
   Fox with glee.
'You really are the very best a Badger friend
   could be.'
Then to his house he hurried back with the
   greatest speed,
'Oh Mrs Fox I have some news, the very best
   indeed!'

But Mrs Fox was crying hard, a sight that was
quite rare.
'Oh Mr Fox! Oh what to do? Our pantry's nearly
bare!
Now we can't invite our friends. It's really such
a shame;
Without the food to share with them our lunch
is not the same!

'And I've only told the children and they're
excited so,
But now I have to tell them I'm afraid they
cannot go!'
'Do not worry Mrs Fox, everything will be all
right,
I think I have a cunning plan to help us in our
plight.

'This is the very season when all the crops are
due —
If we gather some together then we can make
a stew.'
'Why, Mr Fox, how clever, but we must work
quite fast
Till everything is ready and we'll have lunch at
last.'

So off they hurried, paw-in-paw, both searching
    high and low
Until they found the special place where all the
    veggies grow.
'Look here! I say! Oh Mrs Fox, I've carrots, beans
    and peas.
Can you find me some tomatoes and potatoes if
    you please?'

'I have them now, dear Mr Fox. But something
    else I see,
Some lovely herbs and meaty roots to make the
    stew tasty!'
They picked some blackberries for dessert then
    went to see the Bees
'Dear friends, do you think that you could help
    with honey, if you please?'

Back to their house they ran again and, grabbing
    up their pot,
Out on their lawn they made a fire and safely
    cooked the lot!
And just in time, as coming from the other house
    they saw
The Badger family, strolling down and waving
    with their paws.

'Hello you Foxes! Oh how busy you two must
    have been.
What tasty food! What great delights! The best
    we've ever seen!'
And then they ate and sang and danced, having
    great fun all the while,
Then Mr Fox looked to his wife, who gave a
    happy smile.

PETER AND THE CLOCKWORK OWL

On a bright and sunny morning in the house of
   Mr Fox
His eldest child, called Peter, was pulling on his
   socks.
It was just that very morning as the sun began
   to yawn
That little Robin Pippin had woken him at dawn.

So up he'd jumped, but quietly, so as not to
   wake the rest
And thanked his friend the Robin, then quickly
   he got dressed.
Today it was his fishing day. It was his turn
   now to see
If he could catch fish by himself and feed the
   family.
He'd been out fishing lots before but never on
   his own,
He'd always gone with his father, who'd taught
   him all he'd known.

So picking up his fishing rod he slipped now
   from the house
On tippy-toes, in Welly boots, as quiet as any
   mouse.
The other birds were singing now in chirps that
   seemed to say,
'Good morning to this gorgeous day! Hip Hip!
   Hip Hip! Hooray!'

He made his way down to the stream to where
he'd fished before,
Where his father had shown him that there were
fish galore.
He settled down beneath a tree with sunlight
all around,
It shimmered through the leaves above then
danced upon the ground.

The silver stream that passed below went bubbling
on its way
And brought the fishies straight to him, 'Oh
what a fishing day!'
At first one fish, and then two more, then more
still bit his line.
'Our bellies really will be full! On fishies we
shall dine!'

He really felt quite sleepy now so leant back on
his tree
To shut his eyes for forty winks and dream of
fish for tea.
No sooner had he closed his eyes than something
hit his head;
A hazelnut had fallen down. 'Ooh, what was
that?' he said.

Seeing the nut upon the floor, he looked up to
   the tree,
'This is where that nut came from that fell on top
   of me.'
And as he looked up to the tree something shiny
   caught his eye,
Between the branches and the leaves it shimmered
   way up high.

Now as he sat there wondering what could that
   object be,
He heard a faint 'Twit Twit Twoo. Oh, could you
   please help me?'
The voice he heard came from above, from atop
   the tree so tall,
'Oh help me please get down from here. I'm
   scared that I might fall.'

'Oh I will help you,' Peter said. 'And get you
   back down here.
Just hold on tight to where you are. You have
   no need to fear.'
So up he went but carefully, Peter began to
   climb
Slowly now, right to the top, just one branch at
   a time.

And when he finally reached the top, with shock
  he gave a growl,
For clinging to a fat branch sat the silveriest,
  shiniest owl!
His eyes were huge like saucer plates and in
  his belly a clock
His silver wings flapped up and down while his
  tummy went *tick tock*!

'Don't flap your wings now,' Peter said. 'You're
  really up quite high.
I'll try my best to help you down. Unless, of
  course, you fly?'
'Oh deary me!' the owl replied. 'I only wish I
  could!
But though my wings flap up and down, for
  flying they're no good!'

'For I'm a clockwork owl you see,' the owl began
  to cry.
'Each part of me was made by hand but never
  meant to fly.
In my back you'll see a key which, once it has
  been wound,
Will let my clock keep its *tick tock* and help the
  hands turn round.

'It also helps my silver wings flap up and down
  once wound
But not enough to let me fly back safely to the
  ground.'
'Don't worry now,' young Peter said, 'soon you'll
  be safe and sound,
For I will guide you down from here till you're
  on firmer ground.

'Now take a step, then two steps more until
  you're near to me,
Then branch by branch we'll climb back down,
  but slow and carefully.'
So Clockwork Owl he tried his best but really
  had no luck,
For as he reached the fourth branch down he
  found that he was stuck!

'Oh deary me!' poor Owl then cried. 'It's harder
  than we thought
For I cannot reach the branch below. My legs
  are far too short!'
And try as hard, as hard they could, there really
  was no way
To help him reach that next branch down. 'Up
  here I'll have to stay!'

'Hang on there Owl, I have a plan. You must
    do what I say,
It really is the best idea. There is no other way.
Now down below there is a stream, and when
    you hear me shout
I want you to jump straight in – and I will fish
    you out.'

Now, Clockwork Owl he was quite scared but
    gave a little nod
While Peter climbed back down again and grabbed
    his fishing rod.
'Jump now Owl!' Peter shouted out, and in a
    silver flash
Clockwork Owl came hurtling down and landed
    with a splash!

Now Peter drew back with his rod and made a
    little wish,
Then casting out his hook and line he caught
    Owl like a fish!
He hauled him up upon the bank, ooh as heavy
    as can be,
And let him dry there in the sun while he sat
    beneath the tree.

Owl flapped his wings and checked his clock
   then turned his head right round
So he could see he was all there from head right
   down to ground.
'I thank you from my clockwork heart for saving
   me today,
I do not know what I'd have done if you'd not
   passed my way.'

'That's all right, but tell me Owl,' said Peter
   curiously,
'Where is it that you're really from? And why
   were you in that tree?'
'I come from somewhere far from here,' Owl
   answered quietly,
'It's called an Antique Shop, my friend, and sells
   strange things like me.

'It all began quite late last night as light began
   to fail,
We gathered round Grandfather Clock to hear
   him tell his tale,
He told us of a magic wood in a land far, far
   away,
Where every dream was possible and every wish
   a day.

'This story it went round my head as I went to
  bed that night
And wished I was in that fair wood beneath its
  magic light,
For all I had was just one wish, and that was
  to be real,
No more to be a Clockwork Owl but a bird, to
  fly and feel.

'I must have fallen off to sleep as far as I can
  see,
But when I woke at morning time I was on top
  of that tree!'
'Oh what a tale!' young Peter said. 'But what
  now next to do?
I think that you should meet my friend. He'd
  love to meet you too.'

So Peter he packed up his fish then gathered
  up his rod
And deep into the woods beyond the two new
  friends now trod.
At last they reached an old oak tree that had
  a little door
Just above the first small branch but quite far
  off the floor.

'This is the home of Edward Owl,' young Peter
    whispered low.
'When answers will not come to you it's to him
    that you should go.'
'Oh, and he's real!' cried Clockwork Owl, jumping
    excitedly,
'He could teach me how to act just how an owl
    should be!'

'Good morning Edward!' Peter called. 'I have a
    friend for you,
Someone I feel that you should meet and maybe
    help him too.'
They heard a knock and then a bang. The door
    then opened wide
And out stepped Edward Owl himself, 'Here I
    am!' he cried.

He flew down from the branch above and settled
    on the ground.
'Tell me now your young friend's tale and answers
    will be found.'
So Peter told Edward the tale about the Clockwork
    bird,
Who listened very patiently to every spoken
    word.

'Well now, my friend, said Edward Owl, 'I have
  some answers here
That might help you to understand and make
  things seem more clear.
Grandfather Clock told you a tale about a magic
  wood –
This is that very magic place in which we now
  are stood.

'That wish you made, dear Clockwork Owl, you
  wished with all your might,
Was carried to our magic wood on fairy winds
  that night.
You wished so hard to be here, friend, it's plain
  for me to see,
Your wish it carried you to us and put you in
  that tree.'

Clockwork Owl he was so pleased his head turned
  all the way.
'I'm in that very magic wood and here I'll always
  stay!'
But then he looked a little sad. Edward said,
  'What's wrong my dear?'
'Well, I almost had forgotten why I wanted to
  be here.

'I've only ever had one wish and that was to be real,
No more to be a Clockwork Owl but a bird, to fly and feel.'
And just as he had said those words there was a sparkling light,
It shimmered all round Clockwork Owl and hid him out of sight.

But very soon the light had dimmed. 'Oh look!' young Peter said,
For standing there no Clockwork Owl but a real owl now instead!
At first he slowly blinked his eyes then once again, quite fast,
'Oh tell me is it really true? Oh, am I real at last?'

'You are indeed,' said Edward Owl, 'your wish it has come true
And now I think the time has come to do what all owls do.'
So the new Owl fluffed his feathers up and winked an owly eye,
'Yes, I think it's time for me to see if I can really fly!'

So up and down he flapped his wings and slowly
  now he saw
That as he flapped both up and down, he rose
  up from the floor.
And with a whoop of purest joy he flew towards
  the sky
Up and up the owl then flew till he was up
  quite high.

Then down he swooped on gentle breeze and
  landed at their feet.
'At last I am a flying bird. My life is now
  complete!'
'Just one more thing though,' Edward said, 'I
  think you need a name.
We cannot call you Clockwork now. You're really
  not the same.'

'Well, what about Ollie the Owl?' said Peter with
  a smile,
'I think it suits him very well. It has a certain
  style!'
'Yes I love it!' the real Owl said. 'I'm Ollie from
  now on.
The ticking Clockwork side of me now truly has
  all gone!

'And thank you so, my two new friends,' said
  Ollie Owl with glee,
'Now I can live here in this wood forever, happily!'
So Peter Fox with beaming smile went to his
  family
To share his tale, a new best friend and stacks
  of fish for tea!

ANNE FOX AND THE UNICORN

Anne Fox was watching from her house just
   looking at the day,
The clouds had gathered rather fast and looked
   a dismal grey.
At first some drops, just one, two, three and
   then four, five and more,
Until at last in one big sheet the rain began to
   pour.

Now far away she heard a sound and the air
   felt rather warm,
A rumble, grumble, rolling noise. Here comes a
   thunder storm.
'Oh dear,' said Anne, who looked quite stern.
   'This really is not good!
How can I help my Mummy now and go out in
   the woods?'

Just that morning Mrs Fox had said that she
   would try
To make their very favourite thing, a juicy
   mushroom pie.
'All I need,' said Mrs Fox, 'are mushrooms from
   the wood.
Could you help me dearest Anne? I'd be happy
   if you could.'

'Of course dear Mother,' Anne replied. 'I know
which ones to pick,
The ones you showed are safe to eat and will
not make you sick.'
And now the rain had stopped her plans. Oh
would it rain all day?
But as she waited patiently it slowly went away.

The rain it turned to finest mist, the clouds they
floated by,
Until from grey to white to clear, the very bluest
sky.
'I'm off now Mother,' Anne called out. 'I'll take
your basket too
Which I will fill with mushrooms full and bring
them back for you.'

So Anne skipped off into the woods, the sunlight
dancing down
And sparkling bright like diamond light on
raindrops on the ground.
'Oh my,' said Anne as she skipped on, 'where
once was dullest grey
Now the woods are sunny bright – it's such a
lovely day!'

She carried on until she found the place where
    mushrooms grew,
The place her mother had shown her – and only
    those two knew.
Then as she filled her basket full of mushrooms
    from the ground
She heard the very strangest thing, the very
    oddest sound.

What this sound was made from at first she
    couldn't say,
It was a noise that was quite faint and came
    from far away.
She moved off now towards the sound. 'Oh what
    could that noise be?
It goes from low to high and back and sounds
    so sad to me.'

And as she moved on nearer still the sound
    became more clear.
'Oh no! How sad!' Anne cried out loud. 'It's crying
    I can hear.'
She moved through to a clearing now and found
    the crying's source,
For lying there in shafts of light was the smallest,
    whitest horse.

But … this horse was like no other Anne had
  yet seen born,
For there right from his forelock grew the
  squirliest, straightest horn.
The horn itself was very straight and almost
  glowing grey
From thicker base to pointy tip, but twisted all
  the way.

It really did make Anne feel sad to hear the
    poor horse cry.
'Don't be so sad, oh little one. Your tears for you
    I'll dry.'
The little creature raised its head but didn't
    even rise,
He didn't run or turn to move, just looked with
    saddest eyes.

So Anne took out her handkerchief, her clean
    one for that day,
And moved in close to dry his eyes and pat his
    tears away.
He stopped his crying, just a bit, enough to say,
    'Thank you',
But started looking sad again and all his tears
    renewed.

'Oh, what is wrong dear little one? Why are you
    crying so?
What has made you so upset and will not let
    you go?'
'Oh dear,' the little creature sobbed, 'and what
    is really bad,
Is I have lost my Mummy now and I feel very
    sad.'

'Please don't cry, and tell me now where did you
    see her last?
And how it was that she's not here? And what
    has come to pass?'
'Well you see,' the creature said, whose tears
    Anne once more dried,
'We were walking in the woods and I was by
    her side.

'We were eating blackberries, for they are my
    favourite treat,
The juicy ones that are quite black are what I
    love to eat.
But then I heard a mighty *Bang!* and the ground
    beneath me shook,
I got so scared just standing there I wouldn't
    even look.

'I shut my eyes and ran quite fast and further
    on and on
Until I stopped where we are now – and my
    Mummy was gone!'
'Don't cry again, oh little one. We will search
    around
And all my friends will help us till your Mummy
    has been found.

'And don't you worry, little horse, never have
     such fear,
For that loud bang that you had heard would
     never hurt you here.
All it is that made that noise is thunder in the
     sky—
The clouds, all heavy with their rain, bump
     heads as they pass by.'

So Anne she called out to the Bees, who were
     never far away,
And told them now to spread the news whilst
     searching through the day.
And so the Bees they told the Birds, who in
     turn told the Mice,
Who said they would be glad to help and wouldn't
     it be nice.

And so the friends they searched from high and
     some from way down low,
While Anne went with the little horse to judge
     which way to go,
Until at last, from high above, the Birds saw
     down below
The Mummy horse not far from them and flew
     to let them know.

Anne hurried with the little horse to where his
Mummy stood.
The Birds flew low to guide their way and help
them through the wood.
The Mice they cleared the undergrowth to speed
their progress through,
While whistling out their favourite tune and
marching two-by-two.

And then at last a sparkling light came dazzling
from afar
A sparkly, dazzly, glowing light, as bright as any
star.
They hurried on towards its shine, it brightened
up their way,
And walked into a clearing bright, lit up like
lightest day.

And there before them stood a horse, as big as
big can be,
Her horn a shaft of star-bright light, lit up for all
to see.
She stood so proud, her head held high, her coat
as white as snow,
It bounced the light right out again and made
the clearing glow.

Then when at last she turned her head and saw
  her little boy,
She shook her mane and whinnied loud and
  smiled with purest joy.
She kissed and licked and hugged him tight, as
  tight as tight she could,
'I've searched both high and low for you; I thought
  you'd gone for good.'

'Oh Mummy,' said her little boy, 'I really love
  you too.
I am so sorry I got lost and I could not find
  you,
But Mummy this dear little Fox she kindly dried
  my tears,
And helped me find my way to you and calmed
  me and my fears.'

'It was the thunder roar you see. It made him
  scared,' said Anne.
'He was so frightened from the sound he closed
  his eyes and ran.'
'Oh thank you dear,' his Mummy said, 'for bringing
  back my son.
One minute he was by my side, then when I'd
  turned – he'd gone.'

'Oh that's all right, but my dear friends they
    all helped me too,
Together we all helped your horse and brought
    him safe to you.'
'Well, well, my dear he is no horse and neither,
    child, am I,
And those tears that you wiped away held magic
    from each eye.

'For we are Unicorns, my child. Our horns hold
    magic light,
It's goodness that is shining out to help change
    wrongs to right.'
'But may I ask?' said Anne quietly, 'why is your
    son's horn grey?
Is it just that he was sad and missed you so
    today?'

'Well yes, my child, it was his tears. They drained
    the light right out,
But soon his horn will shine again of that I'm
    in no doubt.
And now for all your kindness, dear, I think
    that you should know
That each tear that you wiped away will also
    start to glow.

'For each tear that you wiped away was magic
through and through
And filled with health and happiness and other
good things too,
So if you ever feel unwell, or anyone you know,
Just take a little glowing tear and all sickness
will go.'

'Oh thank you Madam!' Anne cried out. 'I don't
know what to say.
That really is a precious gift you've given me
today.'
'Well now, dear Anne, we have to go, but thank
you all once more,
I have my son back by my side to love and to
adore.'

And in a blink, less than a wink, before their
very eyes
A rainbow-bridge sprang from the ground and
arched up to the skies.
The Unicorns with one last wave, both horns
now shining bright,
Galloped along that rainbow-bridge and up, up,
out of sight.

The Birds, the Mice, the Bees and Anne all
   watched the rainbow fade,
Each one of them so proud about the part each
   friend had played.
Then Anne took out her handkerchief, quite
   gently with her paw,
And sure enough, there glowing, were one hundred
   tears or more.

'And now, my friends, I thank you so for all
   your help once more,
And know if you are sad or sick, you must make
   for my door.'
Then Anne went back to her basket and hurried
   on her way
With mushrooms, wishes and great tales on this,
   a wondrous day!

MARY FOX'S SPECIAL DAY

On a cold and frosty morning in the house of
  Mr Fox
His youngest daughter Mary was laying out her
  frocks.
'Dear Mother,' called out Mary, 'what shall I
  wear today?
My pretty dress with flowers or my woolly dress
  that's grey?'

'Oh Mary wear the warmest one, the grey dress
  if you please,
For outside is so bitter cold I don't want you to
  freeze.'
So Mary dressed with this in mind, wrapped up
  the warmest way,
Prepared at last to go outside and face the
  winter's day.

'Goodbye dear Mother,' Mary said, 'I'm off right
  now to play
But before I go I'll let you know how strange I
  feel today.'
'Oh Mary! What is wrong my dear?' her mother
  turned and said,
'I hope it's not a cold you have – or else right
  back to bed!'

'Oh no dear Mother, not like that. I really don't
    feel ill,
But when I woke I felt it then and yet I feel it
    still,
Today will be a special day, I really know not
    how
I'm sure it's something magical – and will it
    happen now?'

'Well, well, my child,' her mother said, 'you'll
    have to wait and see,
You really are a special child, as special as can
    be.'
So off she went then to explore, watching all
    the way
Lest some surprise should cross her path on
    this, her special day.

Her brother and her sister, Anne, were playing
    just outside.
'Hello you! Come play with us!' her older sister
    cried.
'Thank you so, my sister dear, oh I would love
    to play
But I have the strangest feeling that today's a
    special day.'

So off she went into the woods to a clearing
that she knew,
Where springy moss, all bright and green, beneath
an old oak grew.
She settled down upon the moss and waited
there to see
If any little special thing might happen round
her tree.

She waited and she waited till her eyes began
to close
Then into the moss she snuggled down and there
began to doze.
At first she felt a tickle on the tip of her small
nose
And then she felt another, but kept her eyes
shut closed.

At first she opened one and then the other eye,
But above her all that she could see were branches
and dark sky.
She very slowly sat up straight but could not
believe her eyes,
For all around beyond her tree, the very best
surprise!

Someone had placed a blanket of white stuff all
  around,
Her little clearing sparkled like diamonds on
  the ground.
And as she sat there staring she let out a little
  sigh,
But the magic had not ended as more white
  came from the sky!

Fluffy little white dots came tumbling through
  the air,
They danced a magic hop-scotch, darting here
  and everywhere,
Then when they landed on the ground, this is
  what she liked the best,
They laid upon that blanket there and added to
  the rest!

'I wonder why no white stuff has fallen down
  on me?'
But looking at the tree above, 'twas plain as
  plain can be
The branches of the oak tree were thick and
  grew quite tight,
So except a little tickle here, they shielded out
  the white.

She jumped right up upon her feet, excited now
  to see
What was this white thing made of? Oh whatever
  could it be?
So at first she lifted one foot, then slowly put
  it down.
The white was soft and crunchy yet powdery on
  the ground.

She now put down her other then jumped up
  in the air
And landed down deep in the white as hard as
  she might dare.
Lots of fluffy white flakes came flying all around,
They danced a swirl around her face then floated
  slowly down.

Some tiny little white dots had landed on her
  face,
At first a tickle, then quite cold, to melt without
  a trace.
She bent down now to touch the white, of course
  it would be cold,
But Mary still took off her gloves so the white
  she could now hold.

Her first real touch gave her a shock. 'Oh! Cold
as cold can be!
But look now how it disappears and melts away
from me!'
So more white flakes she gathered up and then
she grabbed some more,
Till pressing hard she'd made a ball and threw
it from her paw!

It hurtled fast right through the air, up high
then way down low
Where the ball was meant to land she really
didn't know.
She watched the ball but then, too late! For who
now did she see?
But Berty squirrel swinging down and coming
from his tree.

Poor Berty did not see the ball while hurrying
down to play,
As freezy-white and fluffy cold came hurtling
fast his way!
Mary let out a little shriek, too late to warn
her friend,
As the frosty-white and fluffy ball now knocked
him on his end!

'I am so sorry!' Mary said. 'I did not see you there,
I did not mean for that at all or to give you such a scare!'
Berty smiled and jumped back up. 'Don't worry Mary dear,
Let's play together in this white and have fun while we're here!'

And so the friends began to play and had the greatest fun
Just throwing white stuff in the air and ball-fights on the run.
Mary laughed and then she asked: 'What could this white stuff be?'
'Oh, I don't know,' replied her friend, 'it's all so new to me.'

'I think it's getting late, Berty. I really have to go.
I'll find out what this whiteness is, my mother ought to know.'
She hugged her friend and headed off, so pleased with her fine day,
Excited now to tell her tale she hurried on her way.

The strangest thing that she then found as she
  moved back to the wood
Was all the white had gone away, no trace, right
  where she stood.
She looked right back from where she'd come
  and saw to her delight
That all the white around her tree was still
  there, shining bright!

'I knew this was a special day! I knew that I
  was right!
Such magic round my little tree with white stuff
  shining bright!'
She burst into her family home, she'd run back
  all the way,
And told them of her magic tale on this, her
  special day.

'Oh yes, dear Mary,' her mother said, 'what you
  saw was snow.
It's only happened once before and that was long
  ago,
It was when I was a little girl on another special
  day,
While I sat beneath that same old oak that you
  sat beneath today.

'But the very saddest thing, my child, is the
magic cannot stay,
For in that very special place it only lasts one
day.'
'Just one day?' her brother said. 'Oh, that is
rather sad.
But Mary what a time you had! Of that I'm
really glad.'

'Oh thank you Peter,' Mary said. 'But what I
now can see,
I wish I'd shared this special day with all my
family.'
'Hang on, my child,' her mother said, 'I think
that we should wait
For Father Fox to come back home, he should
not be too late.

'Then I have a special plan, I'm sure he will
agree:
We'll all go to this magic place, us five, a family.'
And Mary smiled with purest joy, 'Oh, I cannot
wait to play!
Now all of us can share the fun on this, a Special
Day!'